Easy Peasy German!

Your German Phrase Book To Go!

by

Maria Schuster

Table of Contents

History and Introduction

The history of the German Language began in the Early Middle Ages, but since then the German language itself and the German-speaking areas have changed significantly. Today German is the mother tongue of about 120 Million people and mainly spoken in Germany, Austria and the German speaking parts of Switzerland, Luxembourg, Belgium and Italy (South Tirol). As part of the Germanic linguistic group, the German language is distinguished in Low and High German.

In Northern and Central Germany as well as in official Institutions, Schools and Universities of all German-speaking areas only High German is spoken and taught, although lots of dialects have derived from the language and are spoken in many parts of the area as well as in Germany.

Because of Germany's central location in Europe, the German language has been influenced throughout history by many other languages, but especially Latin. But Greek and French, and even a few Slavic languages like Yiddish and Argot affected the transformation of the German language to its current state. Since the 20th century German just like many other languages has been strongly influenced by modern media, with the result of a multitude of Anglicisms.

Today, especially in regards to the IT sector, computers, electronics and technology, English terms are widely spread replacing German words entirely or are being transformed to Anglicisms, which is not always to the liking of traditionally minded German speakers.

For the first time in 1880, a handbook of grammatical and orthographic rules was published by Duden, which was declared as the standard definition of the German language. As languages will continuously evolve and adapt to their speakers based on changing lifestyles, it was astonishing that Duden's Handbook remained essentially unrevised until the reformation of the German language in 1998.

Since then, reformed German spelling as been taught in schools, although traditional spelling co-exist in the Media; for the purpose of this book, we will concentrate on High German as well as on reformed spelling.

Pronunciation and Grammar

Even German speakers will say that learning their native language is difficult. With complex grammar rules, many irregularities and a few instances where simply no rule applies, it can get quite complicated to master all grammar problems right away.

One of the biggest obstacles is the German noun as it has one of three specific grammatical genders - masculine, feminine, or neutral – and is declined for case and grammatical number, which is why German nouns should always be learned with their corresponding definite article – **der**, **die**, or **das**.

Without a doubt the grueling challenge are the German cases. Unlike English, German reflects nouns, adjectives and pronouns in four distinguished grammatical cases – nominative, genitive, dative, and accusative. Plural forms do not just add an "**s**" to the ending of the word, but can end in **-e**, **-en**, **-er**, or even change the vowel of the word.

The German language is a pluricentric language, which means that there is not one consistent pronunciation of the language within the German-speaking area, not even for High German in Germany. Although German has often been referred to by non-Germans as a harsh sounding language, which in part might be due to the guttural pronunciation of a few German diphthong sounds or stem from stereotypical old WWII movies, at a second look the German language reveals many similarities to the pronunciation of the English language and is in some ways much easier.

While the English pronunciation varies between words with similar spelling patterns, in German each diphthong is pronounced consistently – while the diphthong "**ei**" in English words like **ageing, receive** and **beige** changes its pronunciation, "**ei**" in German will always be pronounced as "**eye**".

Vowels can be short or long, but typically they do not change their basic pronunciation like the vowel "**u**" does in **unplugged**, **use** or **urge** – it's always pronounced as "**oo**" in **too**. Most consonants of the German language sound similar to those in English; however, there are a few combinations of consonants that do not exist in the English pronunciation and require a little bit finesse to learn. One example, creating difficulties for non-Germans is the pronunciation of "**ch**" after "**i**" and "**e**", which does not occur in the English language and is pronounced like "**h**" in **huge**.

The German alphabet contains 26 letters and is a so called extended Latin alphabet with the extra letters "**ä**", "**ö**", "**ü**" and "**ß**", whose pronunciation do not really exist in the English language. The following list will show the pronunciation of all German vowels, consonants, diphthongs and digraphs/trigraphs.

<u>Vowels</u>

		English Sound
a		as "**a**" in "father"
e		as "**e**" in "ten"
i		as "**i**" in "dinner"
o		as "**o**" in "cop"
u		as "**ou**" in "you"
ä (ae)		as "**ai**" in "air"
ö (oe)		as "**i**" in "sir"
ü (ue)		as "**y**" in "typical"
y		same as "**ü**" and also as "**y**" in "yacht"

Consonants

		English Sound
b		as "**b**" in "banana"
c		as "**ts**" in "bits" (before "**i**" and "**e**") as "**k**" in "kind"
d		as "**d**" in "dog"
f		as "**ph**" in "phone"
g		as "**g**" in "go"
h		as "**h**" in "help" or silent (after vowels)
j		as "**y**" in "yoga"
k		as "**c**" in "cat"
l		as "**l**" in "love"
m		as "**m**" in "mile"
n		as "**n**" in "nice"
p		as "**p**" in "pig"
q		as "**q**" in "question"
r		as "**r**" in "arm"
s		as "**z**" in "zebra" (before vowels) as "**sh**" in "ship" ("sp", "st", "sch") as "**s**" in "his" (end of syllable/word)
t		as "**t**" in "top"
v		as "**f**" in "father" or as "**v**" in "victory"
w		as "**v**" in "victory"
x		as "**cks**" in "ticks"

| ß | | as "**ss**" in "hiss" |

Digraphs

		English Sound
aa		long "a" sound
ah		as "a" in "bar", longer sound
äh		long "ä" sound
ch		as "ch" in "Loch Ness" (after "a", "o" and "u") as "h" in "huge" (after "i" and "e") as "ch" in "character"
ck		as "ck" in "blocking"
eh		long "e" sound
sch		as "sh" in "shy"
ng		as "ng" in "singing"
ph		as "f" in "fish"
sp		as "sh-p" in "fish pool"
ss		as "ss" in "hiss" (makes the preceding vowel shorter in comparison to "ß")
st		as "sht" in "ashtray"

<u>Diphthongs</u>

		English Sound
au		as "**ow**" in "how"
ai		as "**i**" in "mine"
äu		as "**oy**" in "boy"
ei		as "**i**" in "mine"
eu		as "**oy**" in "boy"
Ie		as "**ee**" in "week"

<u>Everyday Phrases</u>

	Translation	How to say it
Hello.	Hallo	Hah-loh
Good morning.	Guten Morgen	Goo-ten mor-gen
Good day.	Guten Tag	Goo-ten tahk
Good evening.	Guten Abend	Goo-ten ah-bent
Good night.	Gute Nacht	Goo-te nakht
Hi.	Hi	hi
Goodbye.	Auf Wiedersehen Tschüss	owf vee-dair-zayn tchooss
Nice to meet you.	Freut mich!	froyt mikh
How are you?	Wie geht es Ihnen? Wie geht's dir?	vee gayt ess ee-nen vee gayts dear
Fine, thank you.	Danke gut	Dahn-kuh goot
What is your name?	Wie heißen Sie? Wie heißt du?	vee hi-ssen zee vee hiesst doo
My name is.	Ich heiße	ikh hi-ssuh
Yes.	Ja	yah
No.	Nein	nine
Please.	Bitte	bit-tuh

Thank you.	Danke	dahn-kuh
You are welcome.	Bitte schön	bit-tuh shurn
Please, can you help me?	Könnten Sie mir bitte helfen?	kern -ten zee meer bit-tuh hell-fen
Excuse me.	Entschuldigen Sie	ehnt-shool-dih-gun zee
Pardon me.	Entschuldigung	ehnt-shool-dih-goong
I am sorry	Es tut mir leid	ess toot meer lite
Do you speak English?	Sprechen Sie Englisch?	shprekh-en zee eng-lish
Is there someone here who speaks English?	Spricht hier jemand Englisch?	Shprihkht here yeh-mahnd eng-lish
Please repeat that!	Könnten Sie das bitte wiederholen?	kern-ten zee dahs bit-tuh vee-dare-hoh-lan
I understand.	Ich verstehe	ikh fehr-shteh-uh
I do not understand.	Ich verstehe nicht	ikh fehr-shteh-uh nihkht
What does it mean?	Was heißt das?	vahs hi-sst dahs
What time is it?	Wie spät ist es?	Vee spait isst ess
Where is the bathroom?	Wo ist das Badezimmer? Wo sind die Toiletten? (WC)	Voh isst dahs bah-duh-tsimm-err
Where can I find a telephone?	Wo gibt es hier ein Telefon?	Voh geept ess here ine te-le-phone

Accommodation

	Translation	How to say it
Do you have any rooms available?	Haben Sie noch ein Zimmer frei?	Hah-ben zee nokh ine tsimm-err fri
How much is a room for one person?	Wie viel kostet ein Zimmer für eine Person?	Vee feel cost-at ine tsimm-err fewr ine per-zone
How much is a room for two people?	Wie viel kostet ein Zimmer für zwei Personen?	Vee feel cost-at ine tsimm-err fur tsvy per-zone-nan
May I see the room first?	Könnte ich mir das Zimmer erst ansehen?	kern-tuh ikh meer dahs tsimm-err err-st un-zeh- hen
Does the room come with...	Hat das Zimmer…	Haht dahs tsimm-err…
… a bathroom?	… ein Badezimmer?	… ine bah-duh-tsimm-err
… a telephone?	… ein Telefon?	… ine te-le-phone
… bedsheets?	… Bettwäsche?	… bet-wa-shuh
… pillows?	… Kissen?	… kiss-san
… towels?	… Handtücher?	… Hund-tew-kherr
… shower?	… eine Dusche?	… ine-uh doo-shuh
… a TV?	… einen Fernseher?	… i-nan ferrn-zeh-err

Do you have anything...	Haben Sie ein...	Hah-ben zee ine...
... bigger?	... Größeres?	... Grer-sare-ess
... cleaner?	... Saubereres?	... Zau-bear-err-ess
... smaller?	... Kleineres?	... Kline-err-ess
... cheaper?	... Billigeres?	... Bill-eager-ess
... quieter?	... Leiseres?	... Lie-zare-ess
... better?	... Besseres?	... Bess-err-ess
Do you offer...	Haben Sie auch...	... Hah-ben zee au-kh...
... a safe?	...einen Tresor?	... i-nan tra-zore
... lockers?	...ein Schließfach?	... Ine shlee-ss-fahkh
Is breakfast included?	Ist das Frühstück inklusive?	Isst dahs frew-shtyk in-clue-zee-vuh
Is supper included?	Ist das Abendessen inklusive?	Isst dahs ah-bend-ess-san in-clue-zee-vuh
When is breakfast?	Wann gibt es Frühstück?	Vahn gee-pt ess frew-shtyk
When is supper?	Wann gibt es Abendessen?	Vahn geept ess ah-bend-ess-san
Ok, I will take it.	Ok, ich nehme es.	Ok ikh neh-muh ess
I will stay for... night(s).	Ich werde ... Nacht/Nächte bleiben.	ikh vair-duh...naakht/nakh-tuh bli-ben
Can you suggest	Können Sie andere	kern-en zee un-dare-

other hotels?	Hotels empfehlen?	uh hoh-tells em-pha-lan
Please clean my room.	Bitte putzen Sie mein Zimmer.	Bit-tuh put-san zee mine tsimm-err
Could you please wake me at...?	Könnten Sie mich um… wecken?	kern-ten zee mikh uhm …va-can
I would like to check out.	Ich möchte gern auschecken.	ikh *merkh-tuh* gairn aus-check-an

Authorities

	Translation	How to say it
It was a misunderstanding.	Es war ein Missverständnis.	Ess var ine miss-fer-shtand-ness
I haven't done anything wrong.	Ich habe mir nichts zu Schulden kommen lassen.	ikh hah-buh meer nikhts tsoo shull-den com-men lus-san
Am I under arrest?	Nehmen Sie mich fest?	Nah-men zee mikh fest
Where are you taking me?	Wo werde ich hingebracht?	Vo ver-duh ikh hinn-guh-braakht
I want to talk to a lawyer.	Ich will mit einem Anwalt sprechen.	ikh vill mitt i-nam ahn-valt shpra-khan
I am an American / British / Australian / Canadian citizen.	Ich bin Amerikaner / Brite / Australier / Kanadier.	ikh been ameri-cah-nerr / brie-tuh/ ows-traa-lee-err / cah-nah-de-err
I want to talk to the American / British / Australian / Canadian embassy / consulate.	Ich will mit dem amerikanischen / britischen / australischen / kanadischen Konsulat sprechen.	ikh vill mitt dehm ameri-cah-nish-an / brie-tish-an / ows-traa-lish-an / cah-nah-dish-an con-zoo-laat shprai-khan
Can I just pay a fine now?	Kann ich einfach gleich eine Gebühr zahlen?	Cunn ikh ine-fahkh gliekh ine-uh geh-bewr tsah-lan

Bars, Restaurants and Food

	Translation	How to say it
I would like to make a reservation for tonight.	Ich würde gern für heute Abend einen Tisch reservieren.	ikh vewr-duh gairn fewr hoy-tuh ah-bend i-nan tish reh-zer-vee-ran
I would like to make a reservation for tomorrow night.	Ich würde gern für morgen Abend einen Tisch reservieren.	ikh vewr-duh gairn fewr mor-gen ah-bend i-nan tish reh-zer-vee-ran
I have a reservation.	Ich hatte einen Tisch reserviert.	ikh hah-tuh i-nan tish reh-zer- veert
Can I have a table for two please?	Einen Tisch für zwei Personen bitte.	i-nan tish fewr tsvy per-zoe-nan bit-tuh
When is closing time?	Wann schließen Sie?	Vahn shlee-ssan zee
Do you know a good restaurant?	Können Sie ein gutes Restaurant empfehlen?	kern-nan zee ine goo-tas rest-au-runt em-pha-lan
Do you serve alcohol?	Servieren Sie hier alkoholische Getränke?	Zer-vee-ran zee here alcoho-lish-uh geh-tran-cuh
Can we please see the menu?	Könnten wir bitte die Speisekarte sehen?	Kern-ten veer bit-tuh dee shpy-zuh-car-tuh zeh-an
Do you have a children's menu?	Haben Sie ein Kindermenü?	Hah-ben zee ine kinder-manew

What is today's special?	Was ist das Gericht des Tages?	Vahs isst dahs geh-rikht das tah-gas
Is there a house specialty?	Gibt es eine Spezialität des Hauses?	Gibt ess ine-uh shpai-tsia-lee-tait das house-ess
Is there a local specialty?	Gibt es eine Spezialität der Region?	Gibt ess ine-uh shpai-tsia-lee-tait dare reh-ghee-on
What do you recommend?	Was können Sie empfehlen?	Vahs kern-an zee em-pha-lan
Can I look in the kitchen?	Könnte ich einen Blick in die Küche werfen?	kern-tuh ikh i-nan blick in dee kew-khuh ver-fan
A la carte	Von der Speisekarte	fonn dare shpy-zuh-car-tuh
Breakfast	Frühstück	frew-shtyk
Lunch	Mittagessen	Mit-tahk-ess-san
Dinner	Abendessen	ah-bend-ess-an
Supper	Abendessen	ah-bend-ess-an
Salt	Salz	zallts
Pepper	Pfeffer	Pfa-ferr
Black pepper	Schwarzer Pfeffer	Shv-ar-tserr Pfa-ferr
Butter	Butter	Buh-terr
Cream	Sahne	Zaa-neh
Chicken	Huhn	hoon

Fish	Fisch	fish
Ham	Schinken	Shinn-can
Beef	Rind	Rrinnt
Veal	Kalbsfleisch	Culbs-fly-sh
Sausage	Wurst	vurst
Eggs	Eier	Eye-err
Cheese	Käse	Cay-zuh
Salad	Salat	Zaa-laat
Vegetables	Gemüse	Geh-mew-zuh
Fruit	Obst / Früchte	Opsst / frewkh-tuh
Fresh	Frisch	Frish
Toast	Toast	Toast
Bread	Brot	Brroat
Sugar	Zucker	Tsuh-kerr
Rice	Reis	Rrice
Noodles	Nudeln	Noo-delln
Pasta	Nudeln	Noo-delln
Beans	Bohnen	Beau-nan
Tea	Tee	Teh
Coffee	Kaffee	Cah-feh
Milk	Milch	Milkh

Juice	Saft	Zahft
Orange juice	Orangensaft	Orange-an-zahft
Lemon	Zitrone	Tsee-troh-nuh
Soft drink	Limonade	Lee-mo-naa-duh
Ice	Eis	Ice
Coke	Cola	Cola
Water	Wasser	Vahss-err
Bubbly water	Sprudelwasser	Shprew-dell-vahss-err
Tonic water	Tonic	Yonic
Beer	Bier	Beer
Wine	Wein	Vine
White wine	Weißwein	Vice-vine
Red wine	Rotwein	Roht-vine
Whiskey	Whiskey	Vis-key
Rum	Rum	Rrumm
Vodka	Wodka	Vodka
A bottle	Eine Flasche	Ine-uh flush-uh
I am a vegetarian.	Ich bin Vegetarier/in	ikh been veh-geh-tuh-re-err/inn
I don't eat meat.	Ich esse kein Fleisch	ikh ess-uh kine fly-sh

I don't eat pork.	Ich esse kein Schwein	ikh ess-uh kine shvine
I want a dish containing...	Ich möchte eine Speise mit…	ikh merkh-tuh ine-uh shpy-zuh mitt…
I only eat kosher food.	Ich esse nur koscheres Essen.	ikh ess-uh noor kosher-ess ess-an
I'm allergic to...	Ich bin gegen…allergisch	ikh been geh-gen…ah-lair-gish
Waiter!	Ober!	O-ber
Waitress!	Bedienung bitte!	Beh-dee-nung bit-tuh
Excuse me, waiter?	Entschuldigung, Herr Ober?	ehnt-shool-dih-gung hair o-ber
Excuse me, waitress?	Entschuldigung, Bedienung bitte.	ehnt-shool-dih-gung Beh-dee-nung bit-tuh
May I have a glass of...?	Könnte ich bitte ein Glas…bekommen?	Kern-tuh ikh bit-tuh ine glaas…beh-com-man
May I have a cup of...?	Könnte ich bitte eine Tasse…bekommen?	Kern-tuh ikh bit-tuh ine-uh tah-suh…beh-com-man
May I have a bottle of...?	Könnte ich bitte eine Flasche…bekommen?	Kern-tuh ikh bit-tuh ine-uh flash-uh…beh-com-man
Can I have a fork?	Könnte ich bitte eine Gabel bekommen?	Kern-tuh ikh bit-tuh ine-uh gah-bell beh-com-man
Can I have a spoon?	Könnte ich bitte einen Löffel bekommen?	Kern-tuh ikh bit-tuh ine-an lerf-fell beh-com-man

Can I have a knife?	Könnte ich bitte ein Messer bekommen?	Kern-tuh ikh bit-tuh ine mass-ser beh-com-man
Can I have a plate?	Könnte ich bitte einen Teller bekommen?	Kern-tuh ikh bit-tuh ine-an teller beh-com-man
Can I have a glass?	Könnte ich bitte ein Glas bekommen?	Kern-tuh ikh bit-tuh ine glaas beh-com-man
I am hungry.	Ich habe Hunger.	ikh hah-buh hoong-er
I am thirsty.	Ich habe Durst.	ikh hah-buh duhrst
I would like to order.	Ich möchte bestellen.	ikh merkh-tuh beh-shtell-an
I would like a water.	Ich hätte gern ein Wasser.	Ikh ha-tuh gairn ine vuss-ser
I would like a coffee.	Ich hätte gern einen Kaffee.	Ikh ha-tuh gairn ine-an kah-feh
… with milk.	… mit Milch.	Mitt milkh
I would like a tea.	Ich hätte gern einen Tee.	Ikh ha-tuh gairn ine-an teh
…. with lemon.	… mit Zitrone.	Mitt tsee-troh-nuh
I would like an ice tea.	Ich hätte gern einen Eistee.	Ikh ha-tuh gairn ine-an ice-teh
I would like a soft drink.	Ich hätte gern eine Limonade.	Ikh ha-tuh gairn ine-uh lee-moh-naa-duh
I would like a bottle of wine.	Ich hätte gern eine Flasche Wein.	Ikh ha-tuh gairn ine-uh flash-uh vine.

Can you also bring us bread and butter?	Könnten Sie uns auch Brot und Butter bringen?	Kern-tuhn zee oonts owkh brroat oont buht-ter bring-an
What do you have for desserts?	Was haben Sie an Nachtisch da?	Vahs hah-ben ze un nahkh-tish dah
One more, please.	Noch einen / eine bitte.	Nohkh ine-an / ine-uh bit-tuh
Another round, please.	Noch eine Runde bitte.	Nohkh ine-uh ruhn-duh bit-tuh
It was delicious.	Es war sehr lecker.	Ess vahr zehr lack-err
Please clear the plates.	Bitte räumen Sie ab.	Bit-tuh roy-men zee up
Where is the bathroom?	Wo sind die Toiletten?	Voh zind dee toy-lett-an
Please bring me the bill.	Bringen Sie bitte die Rechnung.	Bring-an zee bit-tuh dee rakh-nung

Colors and Numbers

	Translation	**How to say it**
White	Weiß	Vice
Yellow	Gelb	Galb
Orange	Orange	Orange-uh
Red	Rot	Roht
Green	Grün	Grrewn
Brown	Braun	Brrown
Blue	Blau	Blau
Purple	Lila/Violett	Lee-lah/vee-oh-let
Grey	Grau	Grrau
Black	Schwarz	Shvarts
Pink	Rosa	Ro-za
1.	Eins	Ines
2.	Zwei	Tsvy
3.	Drei	Dry
4.	Vier	Feer
5.	Fünf	Fewnf

6.	Sechs	Zecks
7.	Sieben	Zee-bun
8.	Acht	Ahkht
9.	Neun	Noyn
10.	Zehn	Tsayn
11.	Elf	Elf
12.	Zwölf	Tsvurlf
13.	Dreizehn	Dry- tsayn
14.	Vierzehn	Feer - tsayn
15.	Fünfzehn	Fewnf- Tsaen
16.	Sechzehn	Zecks- tsayn
17.	Siebzehn	Zeep-tsayn
18.	Achtzehn	Ahkh-tsayn
19.	Neunzehn	Noyn-tsayn
20.	Zwanzig	Tsvahn-tsikh
21.	Einundzwanzig	Ine-oont-tsvahn-tsikh
22.	Zweiundzwanzig	Tsvy - oont-tsvahn-tsikh
23.	Dreiundzwanzig	Dry - oont-tsvahn-tsikh
24.	Vierundzwanzig	Feer- oont-tsvahn-tsikh

25.	Fünfundzwanzig	Fewnf- oont-tsvahn-tsikh
26.	Sechsundzwanzig	Zecks- oont-tsvahn-tsikh
27.	Siebenundzwanzig	Zee-ben- oont-tsvahn-tsikh
28.	Achtundzwanzig	Ahkht- oont-tsvahn-tsikh
29.	Neunundzwanzig	Noyn- oont-tsvahn-tsikh
30.	Dreißig	Dry-sikh
40.	Vierzig	Feer-tsikh
50.	Fünfzig	Fewnf-tsikh
60.	Sechzig	Zekh-tsikh
70.	Siebzig	Zeep-tsikh
80.	Achtzig	Ahkh-tsikh
90.	Neunzig	Noyn- tsikh
100.	Hundert	Ine-hoon-duhrt
101.	Hunderteins	Hoon-duhrt -ines
200.	Zweihundert	Tsvy- hoon-duhrt
300.	Dreihundert	Dry- hoon-duhrt
400.	Vierhundert	Feer- hoon-duhrt
500.	Fünfhundert	Fewnf- hoon-duhrt

600.	Sechshundert	Zekh- hoon-duhrt
700.	Siebenhundert	Zee-ben- hoon-duhrt
800.	Achthundert	Ahkht- hoon-duhrt
900.	Neunhundert	Noyn- hoon-duhrt
1000.	Tausend	Ine-tow-zuhnt
10,000	Zehntausend	Tsayn- tow-zuhnt
100,000	Hunderttausend	Hoon-duhrt - tow-zuhnt
1,000,000	Eine Million	Ine-uh milli-own
Less.	Weniger	Veh-nee-gerr
Half.	Halb so viel	Halb zo feel
More.	Mehr	Mair

Directions and Transportation

	Translation	How to say it
North	Norden / Nord	Nor-den / Nord
South	Süden / Süd	Zew-den / Zewd
West	Westen / West	Ves-ten / Vest
East	Osten / Ost	Oh-stan / Ohst
Uphill	Bergauf	Bare-g-owf
Downhill	Bergab	Bare-g-up
Left	Links	Links
Right	Rechts	Rakhts
Straight ahead.	Geradeaus	Geh-rah-deh-ows
To the left.	Nach links	Nahkh links
Turn left.	Links abbiegen	Links up-bee-gen
To the right.	Nach rechts	Nahkh rakhts
Turn right.	Rechts abbiegen	Rakhts up-bee-gen
How do I get to...?	Wie komme ich …?	Vee com-muh ikh
... the bus station?	… zur Bushaltestelle?	Tsurr buhs-hahl-tuh-stell-uh
... the airport?	… zum Flughafen?	Tsumm fluhg-hah-fen
... downtown?	… in die Innenstadt?	In dee inn-en-shtaat

... the train station?	... zum Bahnhof?	Tsumm baan-hohf
... the youth hostel?	... ins Hostel / in die Jugendherberge?	Inns hostel / in dee yoo-gant-herr-bear-guh
... the hotel?	... ins Hotel?	Inns hotel
... the embassy?	... zur Botschaft?	Tsure boat-shaaft
... the consulate?	... zum Konsulat?	Tsumm con-zu-laat
Where is the bus/train station?	Wo ist die Bushaltestelle / der Bahnhof?	Voh isst dee buhs-hahl-tuh-stell-uh/ dare baan-hohf
Excuse me, I am looking for the ticket office.	Entschuldigung, ich suche nach dem Fahrkartenautomaten.	ehnt-shool-dih-gung, ikh zoo-khuh nahkh dehm fahr-car-ten-ow-toe-mah-ten
I would like a one way ticket to....	Ich hätte gern eine einfache Fahrkarte nach / zum / zur…	Ikh hai-tuh gairn ine-uh ine-fah-khuh fahr-car-tuh nahkh / tsumm / tsure
I would like a round trip ticket to....	Ich hätte gern eine Fahrkarte für Hin- und Rückfahrt…	ikh hai-tuh gairn ine-uh fahr-car-tuh fewr hinn-oont-rewck-fart
I would like to sit in the smoking car.	Ich möchte im Raucherabteil sitzen.	Ikh merkh-tuh imm rowkh-err-up-tile zit-tsen
I would like to sit in the non-smoking car.	Ich möchte im Nichtraucherabteil sitzen.	Ikh merkh-tuh imm nihkht-rowkh-err-up-tile zit-tsen

Where does this train/bus go?	Wohin fährt dieser Zug / Bus?	Voh-hinn fairt dee-zer tsoog / buhss
Where is the train/bus to...?	Wo fährt der Zug / Bus nach...ab?	Voh fairt dare tsoog / buhss nahkh ... ap
Does this train/bus stop in...?	Hält dieser Zug / Bus in...?	Haillt dee-zer tsoog / buhss in...
What is the departure and arrival time?	Was sind die Abfahrts- und Ankunftszeiten?	Vahs zind dee ap-farts-oont ahn-koonfts-tsy-ten
How much is a first class ticket?	Wie viel kostet eine Fahrkarte in der ersten Klasse?	Vee feel cost-at ine-uh fahr-car-tuh in dare air-stan clah-ssuh
Entrance.	Eingang	Ine-gahng
Exit.	Ausgang	Ows-gahng
Where is the bus stop?	Wo ist die Bushaltestelle?	Voh isst dee buhs-hahl-tuh-stell-uh
One way ticket.	Einfache Fahrkarte	ine-fah-khuh fahr-car-tuh
A round trip ticket.	Hin- und Rückfahrkarte	hinn-oont-rewck-far-car-tuh
Do you go to...	Fahren Sie nach...?	Fah-ran zee nahkh
Do you have a schedule?	Haben Sie einen Fahrplan?	Hah-ben zee ine-an far-plaan
Which direction do I have to go?	In welche Richtung muss ich gehen?	In vel-khuh rihkh-toong mooss ikh geh-hen

How often do the trains run?	Wie häufig fahren die Züge?	Vee hoy-fig fah-ren dee tsew-guh
How many stops are there?	Wie oft hält der Zug?	Vee owft hellt dare tsoog
Please tell me when we get there?	Könnten Sie mir bitte Bescheid sagen, wenn wir da sind?	Kern-ten zee meer bit-tuh beh-shiet sah-gen
How do I get there?	Wie komme ich da hin?	Vee com-muh ikh dah hinn
Where is the closest metro station?	Wo ist die nächste U-Bahnstation?	Voh isst dee nakh-stuh uh-baan-stah-tion
How much is the fare?	Wie viel kostet die Fahrkarte?	Vee feel cost-et dee far-car-tuh
How long does it stop?	Wie lange hält der Zug?	Vee lung-uh hellt dare tsoog
From what platform does it leave?	Von welchem Gleis fährt der Zug?	Fon vel-kham glise fairt dare tsoog
Do I have to change trains?	Muss ich umsteigen?	Mooss ikh uhm-sty-gen
Is this place taken?	Ist dieser Platz besetzt?	Isst dee-zer plaats beh-zetst
How much does it cost?	Wie viel kostet das?	Vee feel cost-et dahs
Where do I get off?	Wo muss ich aussteigen?	Voh mooss ikh ows-sty-gen
What time does the	Wann fährt der Zug	Vahn fairt dare tsoog

train leave?	ab?	ap
Towards the...	In Richtung…	In rihkh-toong
Past the...	Hinter…	Hinn-ter
Before the...	Vor…	for
Street	Straße	Shtrah-suh
Intersection	Kreuzung	Croy-tsoong
One way	Einbahnstraße	Ine-baan- shtrah-suh
No parking	Parkverbot	Park-fer-boat
Gas/petrol station	Tankstelle	Tunk-shtell-uh
Gas/petrol	Benzin	Ben-tsyn
Diesel	Diesel	Dee-zell
Fare	Fahrpreis	Far-price
Speed limit	Höchstgeschwindigkeit	Herkhst-geh-shvin-dig-kite
Taxi!	Taxi!	Taa-xi
Take me to...., please.	Bringen Sie mich bitte nach…	Brring-an zee mikh bit-tuh nahkh
How much does it cost to go to...?	Wie viel kostet es bis…?	Vee feel cost-at ess biss
Take me there, please.	Bitte fahren Sie mich dort hin.	Bit-tuh far-en zee mikh dort hinn
Is there a subway in this city?	Gibt es in dieser Stadt eine U-Bahn?	Geept ess in dee-zer shtaatt ine-uh uh-baan

Where can I buy a ticket?	Wo kann ich eine Fahrkarte kaufen?	Voh cun ikh ine-uh far-car-tuh cow-fen
Do you have a map showing the subway stops?	Haben Sie eine Karte, auf der die U-Bahnstationen eingezeichnet sind?	Hah-ben ze eine car-tuh owf dare dee uh-baan-shtaa-tion-nan ine-geh-tsykh-net zind
Can you show me on the map?	Könnten Sie mir das auf der Karte zeigen?	Kern-ten zee meer dahs owf dare car-tuh tsy-gen
Please take me to this address.	Bitte fahren Sie mich zu dieser Adresse.	Bit-tuh fah-ren zee mikh tsoo dee-zer ah-dress-uh
Is it far from here?	Ist das weit von hier?	Isst dahs vite fon here
I am lost.	Ich habe mich verirrt.	Ikh hah-buh mikh fer-irrt
I want to rent a car.	Ich möchte ein Auto mieten.	Ikh merkh-tuh ine ow-toe me-ten

Emergencies and Problem Phrases

	Translation	How to say it
Help!	Hilfe!	Hill-fuh
What is wrong?	Was ist passiert?	Vahs isst pass-eert
Leave me alone.	Lassen Sie mich zufrieden.	Lass-an zee mikh tsoo-free-den
Don't touch me!	Fassen Sie mich nicht an!	Fass-an zee mikh nihkht un
I will call the police.	Ich werde die Polizei rufen.	Ikh ver-duh dee poh-lee-tsy roo-fen
Police!	Polizei!	Poh-lee-tsy
Stop! Thief!	Stopp! Dieb!	Shtop! Deeb
It's an emergency.	Dies ist ein Notfall.	Dees isst ine note-fahl
I need help.	Ich benötige Hilfe.	Ikh beh-nert-ee-guh hill-fuh
I'm lost.	Ich habe mich verirrt.	Ikh hah-buh mikh fer-irrt

Medical

	Translation	How to say it
I have pain.	Ich habe Schmerzen.	Ikh hah-buh shmare-tsen
I have a stomach ache.	Ich habe Magenschmerzen.	Ikh hah-buh mah-gen-shmare-tsen
I am a diabetic.	Ich bin Diabetiker.	Ikh been dee-ah-beh-ticker
I have backache.	Ich habe Rückenschmerzen.	Ikh hah-buh rewk-an shmare-tsen
I have a toothache.	Ich habe Zahnschmerzen.	Ikh hah-buh tsahn-shmare-tsen
I do not feel good.	Ich fühle mich nicht wohl.	Ikh phewh-luh mikh nihkht wohl
I have chest-pain.	Ich habe Schmerzen in der Brust.	Ikh hah-buh shmare-tsen in dare bruhsst
I had a heart attack.	Ich hatte einen Herzinfarkt.	Ikh hah-tuh ine-an hare-tsinn-farkt
I have cramps.	Ich habe Krämpfe.	Ikh hah-buh kraimp-fuh
I have a sore throat.	Ich habe Halsschmerzen.	Ikh hah-buh hahlts-shmare-tsen
I am allergic to…	Ich bin gegen…allergisch.	Ikh been geh-gen…ah-lair-gish

I need a doctor.	Ich brauche einen Arzt.	Ikh brrow-khuh ine-an artst
I need a dentist.	Ich brauche einen Zahnarzt.	Ikh brrow-khuh ine-an tsarn-artst
I need a nurse.	Ich brauche eine Krankenschwester.	Ikh brrow-khuh ine-uh krun-can-shvas-ter
I feel sick.	Ich bin krank.	Ikh been krunk
I have a headache.	Ich habe Kopfschmerzen.	Ikh hah-buh copf-shmare-tsen
I think that I have the flu.	Ich glaube, ich habe die Grippe.	Ikh glaow-buh ikh hah-buh ine-uh grip-puh
I feel dizzy.	Mir ist schwindelig	Meer isst shvin-dell-ig
I feel nauseous.	Mir ist übel.	Meer isst ew-bell
I have fever.	Ich habe Fieber.	Ikh hah-buh fee-ber
It hurts here.	Es tut hier weh.	Ess toot here vay
Where's a hospital?	Wo ist das Krankenhaus?	Voh isst dahs krun-ken-house

Money

	Translation	How to say it
Do you accept American dollars?	Kann man hier mit US-Dollar bezahlen?	Cunn mahn here mitt us-dollar beh-tsah-len
Do you accept Euros?	Kann man hier mit Euro bezahlen?	Cunn mahn here mitt oy-roh beh-tsah-len
Do you accept British pounds?	Kann man hier mit britischen Pfund bezahlen?	Cunn mahn here mitt brrit-tish-en pfoont beh-tsah-len
Do you accept credit cards?	Kann man hier mit Kreditkarte bezahlen?	Cunn mahn here mitt kreh-deet-car-tuh beh-tsah-len
Where can I find an ATM?	Wo ist der nächste Geldautomat?	Voh isst dare nakh-stuh gelt-aow-toh-maat
Where can I withdraw money?	Wo kann ich Geld abheben?	Voh cunn ikh gelt up-heh-ben
Where is the bank?	Wo ist die Bank?	Voh isst dee bahnk
What is the exchange rate?	Was ist der Wechselkurs?	Vahs isst dare vax-sell-course
Where can I get money changed?	Wo kann ich Geld wechseln?	Voh cun ikh gelt vax-selln
Can you change money for me?	Könnten Sie mir mein Geld wechseln?	Kern-ten zee meer mine gelt vax-selln
Where can I get a	Wo kann ich	Voh cunn ikh rye-zuh-

traveler's check changed?	Reisechecks einlösen?	checks ine-lew-zen
Can you change a traveler's check for me?	Kann ich bei Ihnen meinen Reisecheck einlösen?	Cunn ikh by ee-nan mine-an rye-zuh-check ine-lew-zen

<u>Shopping</u>

	Translation	How to say it
I am looking for a shopping center.	Ich suche nach einem Kaufhaus.	Ikh soo-khuh nahkh ine-am cowf-house
Where can I find a department store?	Wo ist das nächste Kaufhaus?	Voh isst dahs nakh-stuh cowf-house
Where can I find a gift shop?	Wo gibt es hier einen Souvenirshop?	Voh geept ess here ine-an zou-veh-nir-shop?
Where can I find a market?	Wo gibt es hier einen Markt?	Voh geept ess here ine-an markt
Where can I find a clothing store?	Wo gibt es hier einen Klamottenladen?	geept ess here ine-an klah-mot-ten-lah-den
Please show me.	Bitte zeigen Sie es mir.	Bit-tuh tsy-gen zee ess meer
I'd like something.	Ich hätte gern etwas.	Ikh hai-tuh gairn at-vahs
I need...	Ich brauche…	Ikh brrow-khuh
... batteries	… Batterien	Baht-ter-ee-an
… a pen	… einen Stift	Ine-an shtift
... condoms	… Kondome	Con-doh-muh
… change	… Kleingeld	Kline-gelt
… a postcard	… eine Postkarte	Ine-uh posst-car-tuh

... postage stamps	... eine Briefmarke	Ine-uh brreef-mar-kuh
... a razor	... einen Rasierapparat	Ine-an raa-zeer-up-pah-raat
... shampoo	... Haarwaschmittel	Hahr-vahsh-mit-tell
...aspirin	... Aspirin	Ass-pee-reen
... cold medicine	... Medizin gegen Erkältungen	Meh-dee-tseen geh-gen ehr-cal-toong
... stomach medicine	... Medizin gegen Magenschmerzen	Meh-dee-tseen geh-gen mah-gen shmare-tsen
... soap	... Seife	Zei-fuh
... tampons	... Tampons	Tahm-pongs
... writing paper	... Schreibpapier	Shribe-pah-pier
... sunblock lotion	... Sonnencreme	Zon-an-kreh-muh
... toothpaste	... Zahnpaste	Tsaan-paa-stuh
... a toothbrush	... eine Zahnbürste	Ine-uh tsaan-bewr-stuh
... an umbrella	... einen Regenschirm	Ine-an reh-gen-shirm
... English-language books	... englischsprachige Bücher	Eng-lish-shprah-khee-guh bew-kher
... English-language magazines	... englischsprachige Zeitschriften	Eng-lish-shprah-khee-guh tsiet-shriff-ten
... English-language newspaper	... englischsprachige Zeitungen	Eng-lish-shprah-khee-guh tsy-toong-an

Do you take VISA?	Kann man hier mit VISA-Karte bezahlen?	Cunn mahn here mitt VISA-car-tuh beh-tsah-len
Do you take debit cards?	Kann man hier mit Checkkarte bezahlen?	Cunn mahn here mitt check-car-tuh beh-tsah-len
Do you take American dollars?	Kann man hier mit US-Dollar bezahlen?	Cunn mahn here mitt US-Dollar beh-tsah-len
Do you have?	Haben Sie…?	Hah-ben zee
Do you have this in my size?	Haben Sie das in meiner Größe?	Hah-ben zee dahs in mine-err groer-ssuh
Expensive	Teuer	Toy-are
Cheap	Billig	Bill-eager
I'd like to try it on.	Ich möchte es gern anprobieren.	Ikh merkh-tuh ess gairn un-pro-beer-an
It does not fit (me).	Es passt mir nicht.	Ess pahsst meer nihkht
It fits very well.	Es passt gut.	Ess pahsst goot
How much is it?	Wie viel kostet es?	Vee feel cost-at ess
I can't afford it.	Das kann ich mir nicht leisten.	Dahs cunn ikh meer nihkht lie-sten
That is too expensive.	Das ist zu teuer.	Dahs isst tsoo toy-are
You're cheating me.	Das ist doch Betrügerei!	Dahs isst dokh beh-trew-ger-eye
I'd like something	Ich möchte etwas	Ikh merkh-tuh at-vahs

else.	anderes.	ahn-dare-ess
I'm not interested.	Ich bin daran nicht interessiert.	Ikh been dah-run nihkht in-teh-reh-sseert
I don't want it.	Ich möchte es nicht.	Ikh merkh-tuh ess nihkht
I will take it.	Ich nehme es.	Ikh neh-muh ess
Can I have a bag?	Könnte ich eine Tüte bekommen?	Kern-tuh ikh ine-uh tewh-tuh beh-com-men
Can you ship it to my country?	Verschicken Sie ins Ausland?	Fer-shick-an zee inns aows-lund

Time and Date

	Translation	How to say it
Minute / Minutes	Die Minute / Minuten	Dee min-uh-tuh / n
Hour / Hours	Die Stunde / Stunden	Dee shtunn-duh / n
Day / Days	Der Tag / die Tage	dehr tahk/ dee tah-ge
Week / Weeks	Die Woche / Wochen	Dee woh-khe
Month / Months	Der Monat / die Monate	Dehr moh-naht
Year / Years	Das Jahr / die Jahre	Duhs yaar / die yaa-reh
3 o'clock AM	3 Uhr nachts	Dry oor nahkts
8 o'clock AM	8 Uhr	Ahkht oor mor-gen-ts
2 o'clock PM	14 Uhr	tsvy oor nahk-mih-tahks
9 o'clock PM	21 Uhr	Noyn oor ah-bends
Monday	Montag	mohn-tahk
Tuesday	Dienstag	deens-tahk
Wednesday	Mittwoch	mit-vock
Thursday	Donnerstag	don-ers-tahk
Friday	Freitag	fry-tahk
Saturday	Samstag	zahms-tahk

Sunday	Sonntag	zon-tahk
Today	Heute	hoy-tuh
Yesterday	Gestern	geh-stairn
Tomorrow	Morgen	mawr-gun
This Week	Diese Woche	Dee-zuh voh-khuh
Last Week	Letzte Woche	Lets-tuh voh-khuh
Next Week	Nächste Woche	Nakh-stuh voh-khuh
January	Januar	yah-noo-ahr
February	Februar	fay-broo-ahr
March	März	mehrts
April	April	ah-pril
May	Mai	my
June	Juni	yoo-nee
July	Juli	yoo-lee
August	August	ow-goost
September	September	zehp-tehm-ber
October	Oktober	ok-toh-ber
November	November	no-vehm-ber
December	Dezember	deh-tsem-ber
June 13th, 2003	13. Juni 2003	Dry- tsayn-ter yoo-nee tsvy- tow-zuhnt-

		dry
October 21st, 1999	21. Oktober 1999	ine-oont-tsvahn-tsikh-stare ok-toh-ber noyn-tsayn- hoon-duhrt-noyn-oont- noyn-tsikh

I sincerely hope you will get as much pleasure from this phrase book as I have had making it.

Now please go enjoy the beautiful country of Germany with your

newly learned language skills...

Printed in Great Britain
by Amazon